Contents:-

Introduction:-

In this book we will learn about share market candlestick patterns and chart patterns.

Before doing trading in share market we should know about candlestick pattern and chart pattern. With the help of these patterns we can easily trade in share market and make profit.

Candlestick Pattern is a movement in prices shows graphically on a candlestick chart.

Candlestick Patterns (Every Trader should know about these Candlestick Patterns)

Two types of Candlestick Patterns

1. Bullish Candlestick patterns
2. Bearish Candlestick patterns

Now we will learn one by one all candlestick patterns.

Bullish Candlestick:-

Bullish Candle start from low and close at up.

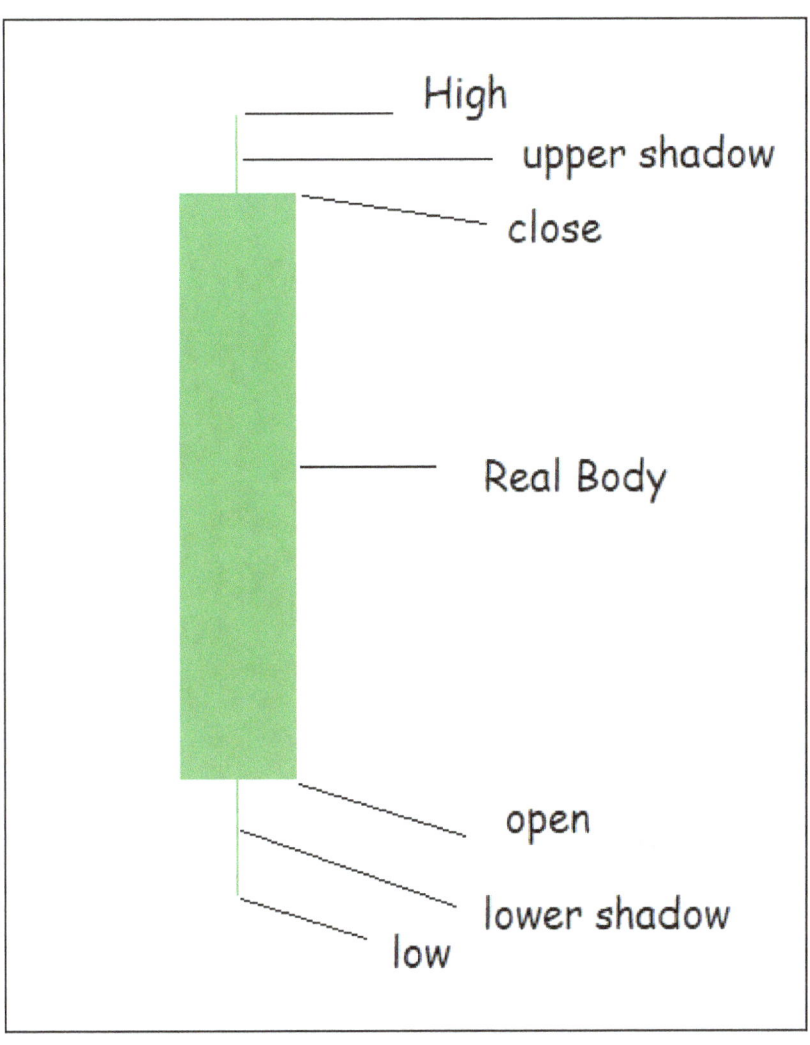

Bearish Candlestick:-

Bearish Candle start from up and close at down.

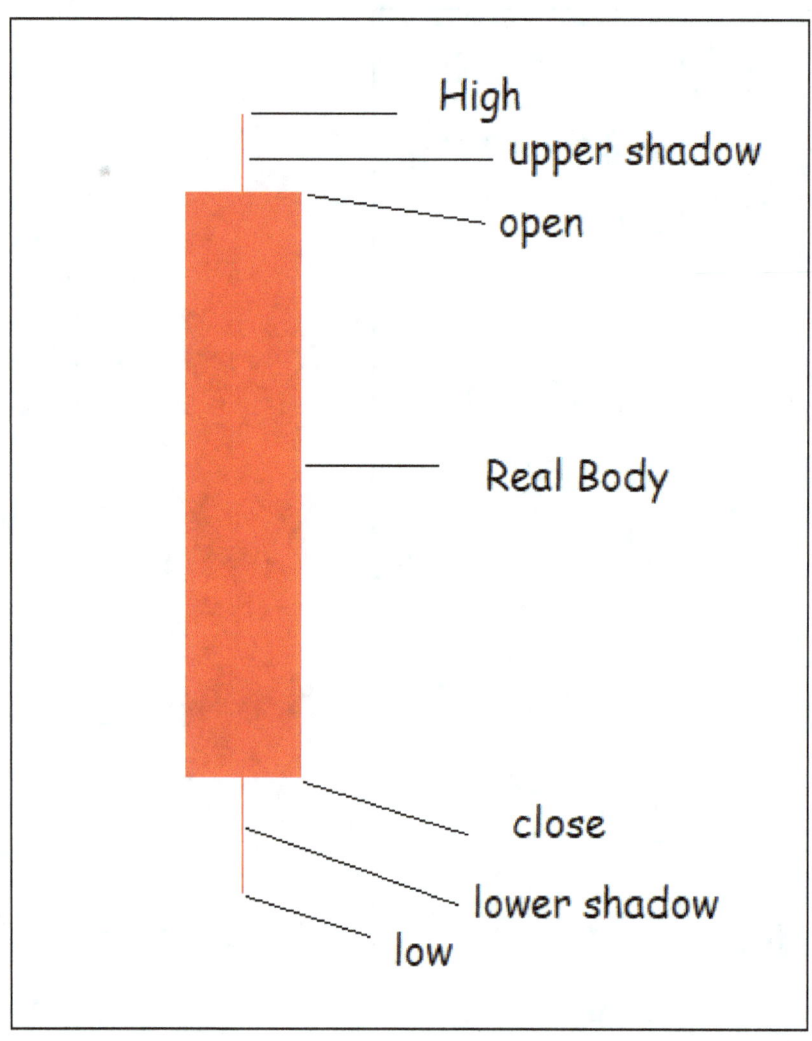

1. Bullish Engulfing Pattern:-

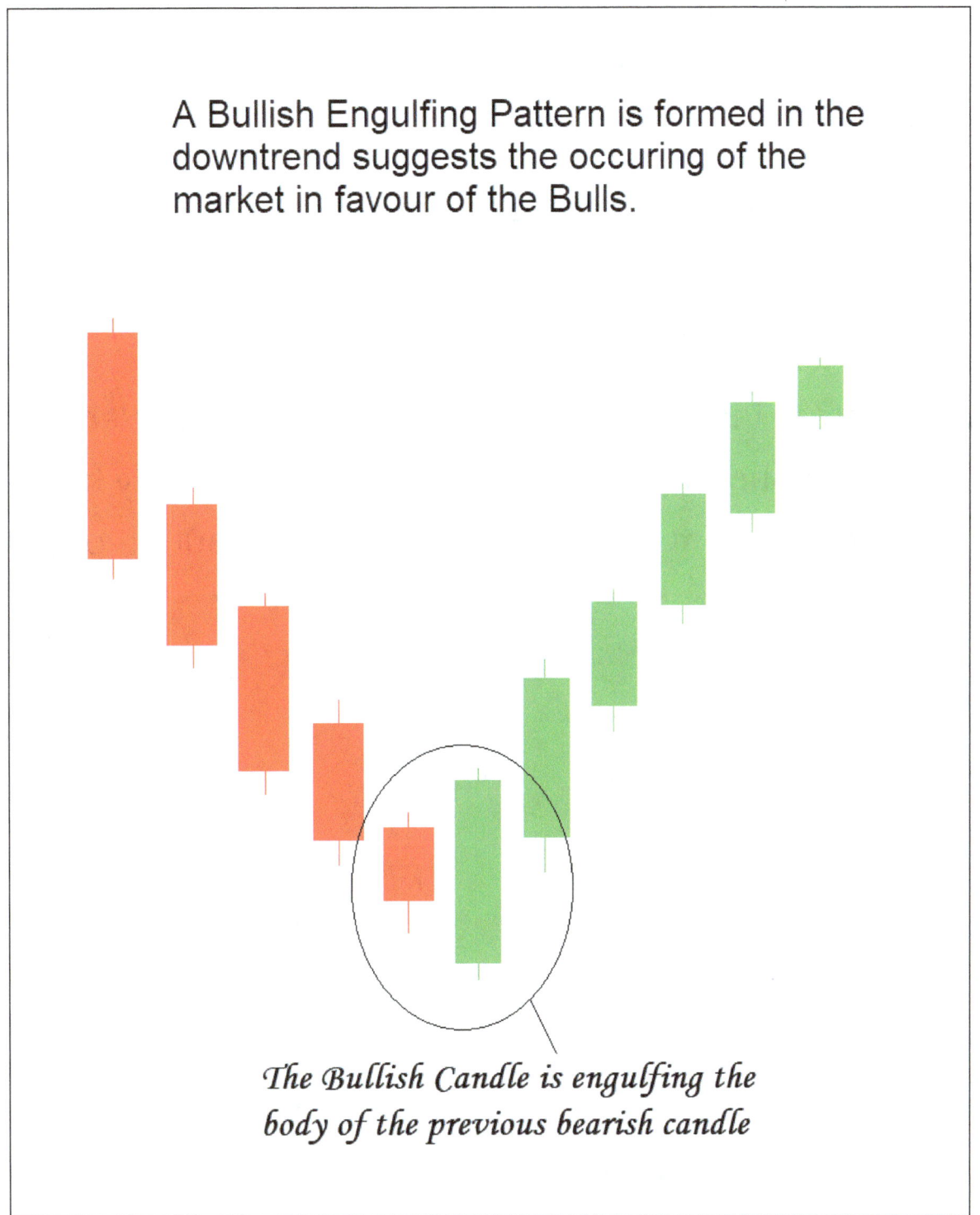

A Bullish Engulfing Pattern is formed in the downtrend suggests the occuring of the market in favour of the Bulls.

The Bullish Candle is engulfing the body of the previous bearish candle

What is a Bullish Engulfing Pattern?

A Bullish Engulfing Pattern is a technical analysis chart pattern that signals a potential reversal from a downtrend to an uptrend.

It consists of two candlestick a small bearish candlestick followed by a larger bullish candlestick that covers the entire body of previous candlestick.

This pattern indicates that buying pressure has overcome selling pressure and suggests that the market may be transitioning from a bearish sentiment to a bullish one.

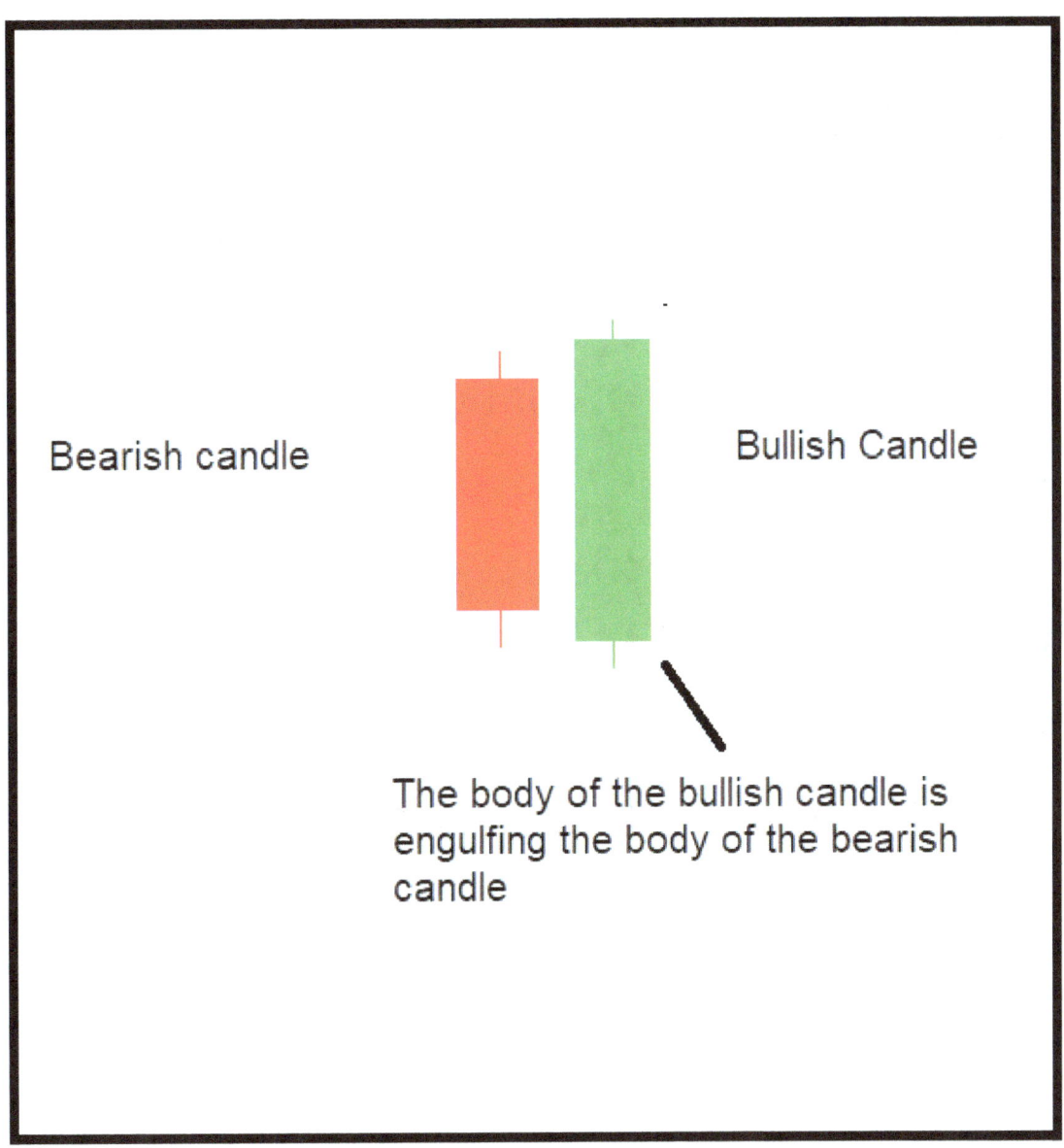

Bearish candle

Bullish Candle

The body of the bullish candle is engulfing the body of the bearish candle

How does a Bullish Engulfing Pattern form?

The market is in a downtrend or at a support level.

A small bearish candle forms representing a continuation of the selling pressure.

The next day the market opens lower than the previous day's closer.

Buyers then enter the market, pushing prices higher throughout the day.

The bullish candle closer above the previous day's open, engulfing the entire body of the bearish candle.

Important Points

Confirmation- Look for additional confirmation signals, such as an increase in trading volume, a break of a trend line etc.

Context- The Bullish Engulfing Patten is more significant if it appears after a prolonged downtrend or at a key support level. It can also carry weight if it forms near a moving average, Fibonacci retracement level, or another technical confluence zone.

Risk Management – As with any trading strategy, proper risk management is essential. Establish a stop-loss order below the pattern's low or at a predetermined level based on your risk tolerance.

False signals- Be aware that the Bullish Engulfing Pattern can occasionally produce false signals. It is crucial to consider the overall market context, additional technical analysis, and other factors before making a trade.

No guarantee – Keep in mind that while the Bullish Engulfing Pattern is a strong indicator of a potential trend reversal, it is not a guarantee. Market conditions can change to adapt their strategies accordingly.

2. Bearish Engulfing Pattern:-

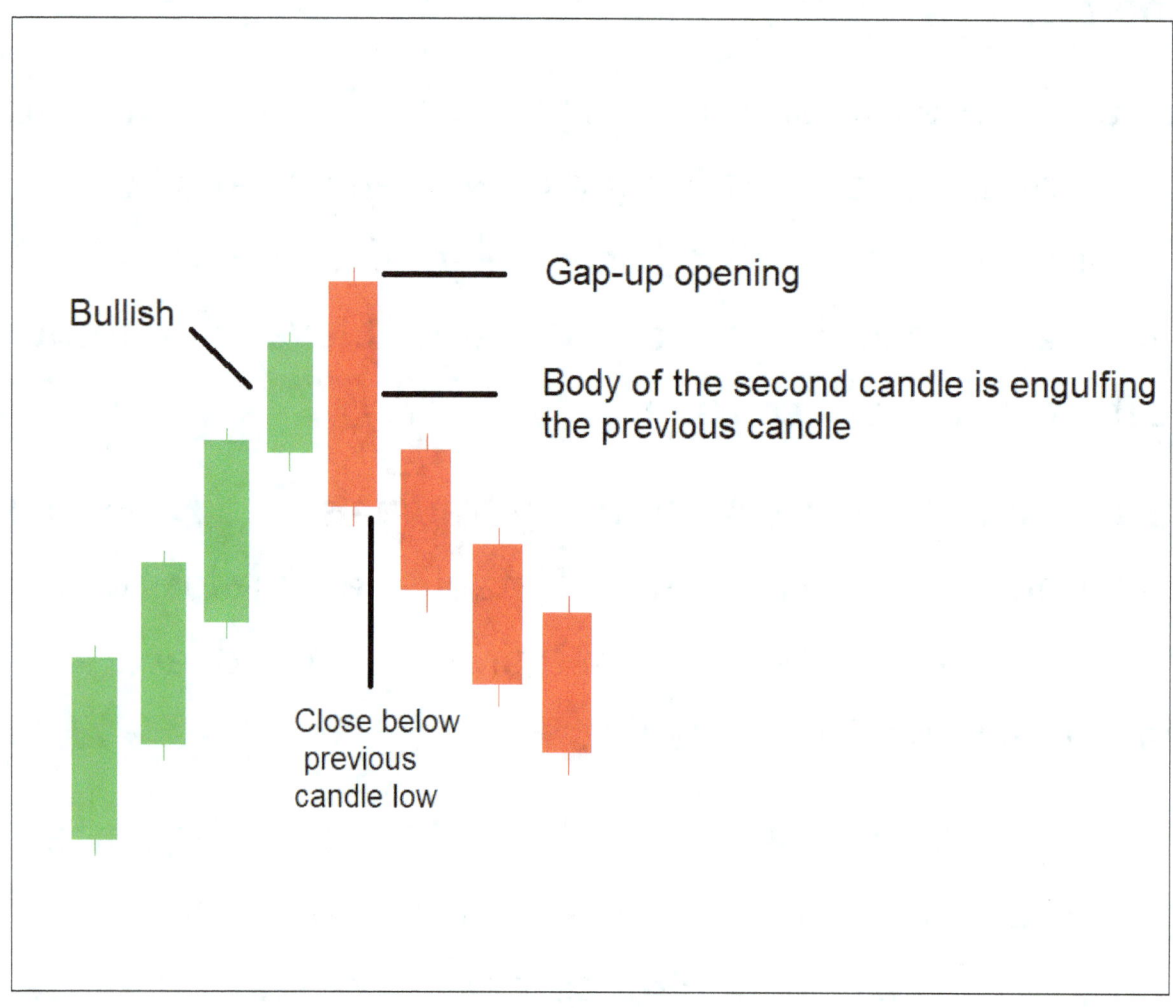

What is a Bearish Engulfing Pattern?

A Bearish Engulfing Pattern is a technical analysis chart pattern used to indicate a potential reversal from an uptrend to a downtrend in the market.

It is a bearish signal, suggesting that sellers are taking control over buyers, and is often used by traders to identify possible short-selling opportunities.

The Bearish Engulfing Pattern forms through a two candle process:

The first candle is a bullish candle with a smaller body indicating that the closing price is higher than the opening price for that period.

The second candle is a bearish candle with a larger body that engulfs the entire body of the previous candle. This indicates that the closing price is the lower than the opening price for the period and the selling pressure has surpassed the buying pressure.

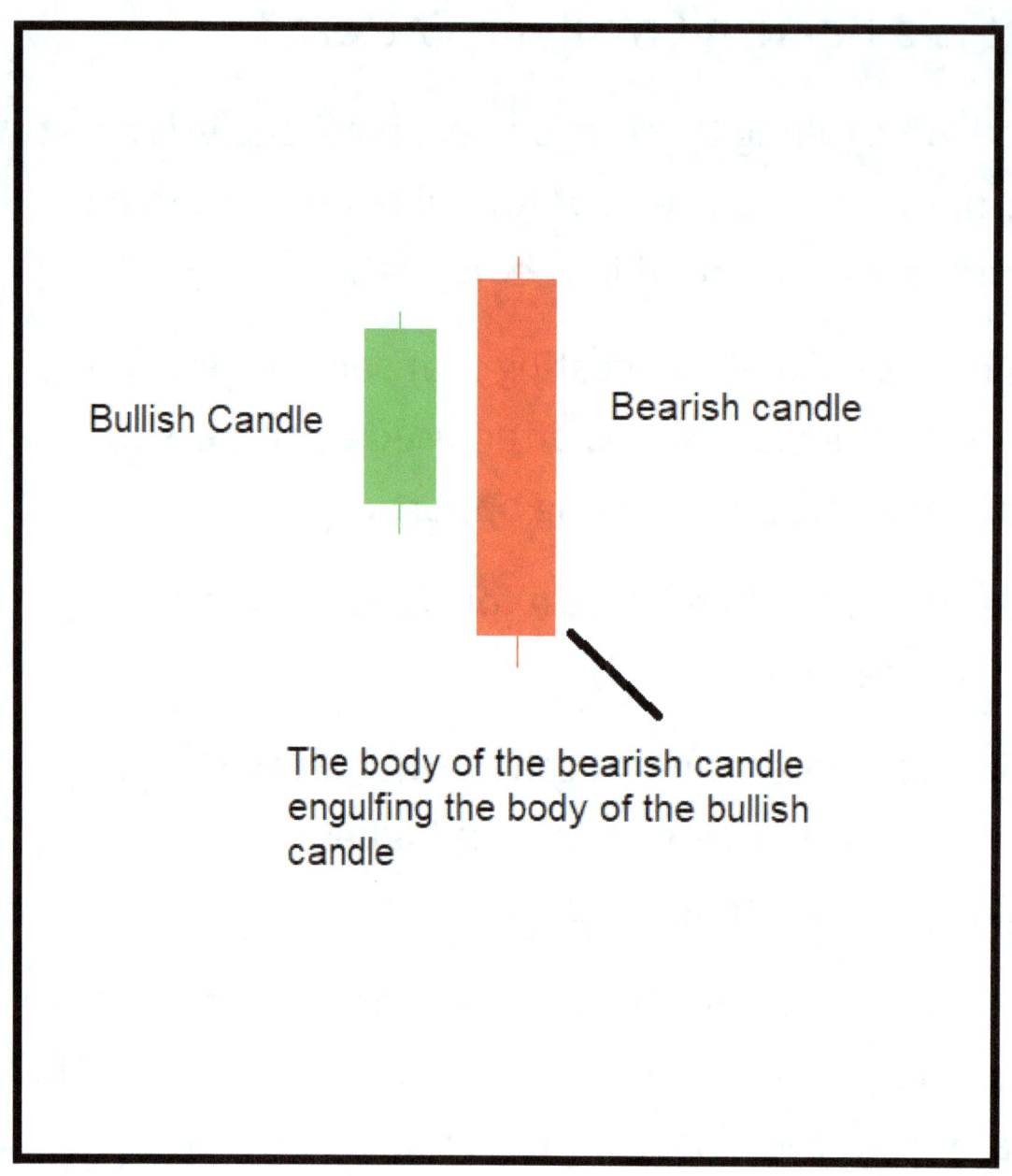

Bullish Candle

Bearish candle

The body of the bearish candle engulfing the body of the bullish candle

The Bearish Engulfing Pattern forms through a two candle process:

The first candle is a bullish candle with a smaller body indicating that the closing price is higher than the opening price for that period.

The second candle is a bearish candle with a larger body that engulfs the entire body of the first candle. This indicate that the closing price is lower than the opening price for the period, and the selling pressure has surpassed the buying pressure.

Important points:-

Confirmation- the Bearish Engulfing Pattern is more reliable when it is followed by additional bearish price action or other confirming technical indicators.

Context- The pattern is most significant when it occurs at the end of an uptrend or after a price rally, as it can signals a trend reversal.

Volume- Increased trading volume during the formation of the bearish engulfing candle can strengthen the pattern's bearish signal.

Support and Resistance- Look for the pattern near key support or resistance levels, as it may indicate a stronger potential reversal.

Timeframe- The Bearish Engulfing Pattern can be observed on various timeframe, but its significance increases on longer timeframes like daily, weekly, or monthly charts.

Remember, while the Bearish Engulfing Pattern is a useful tool for identifying potential reversals, it is essential to use it in conjunction with other technical analysis tools and methods for more accurate trading decisions.

3. Bullish Marubozu candle:-

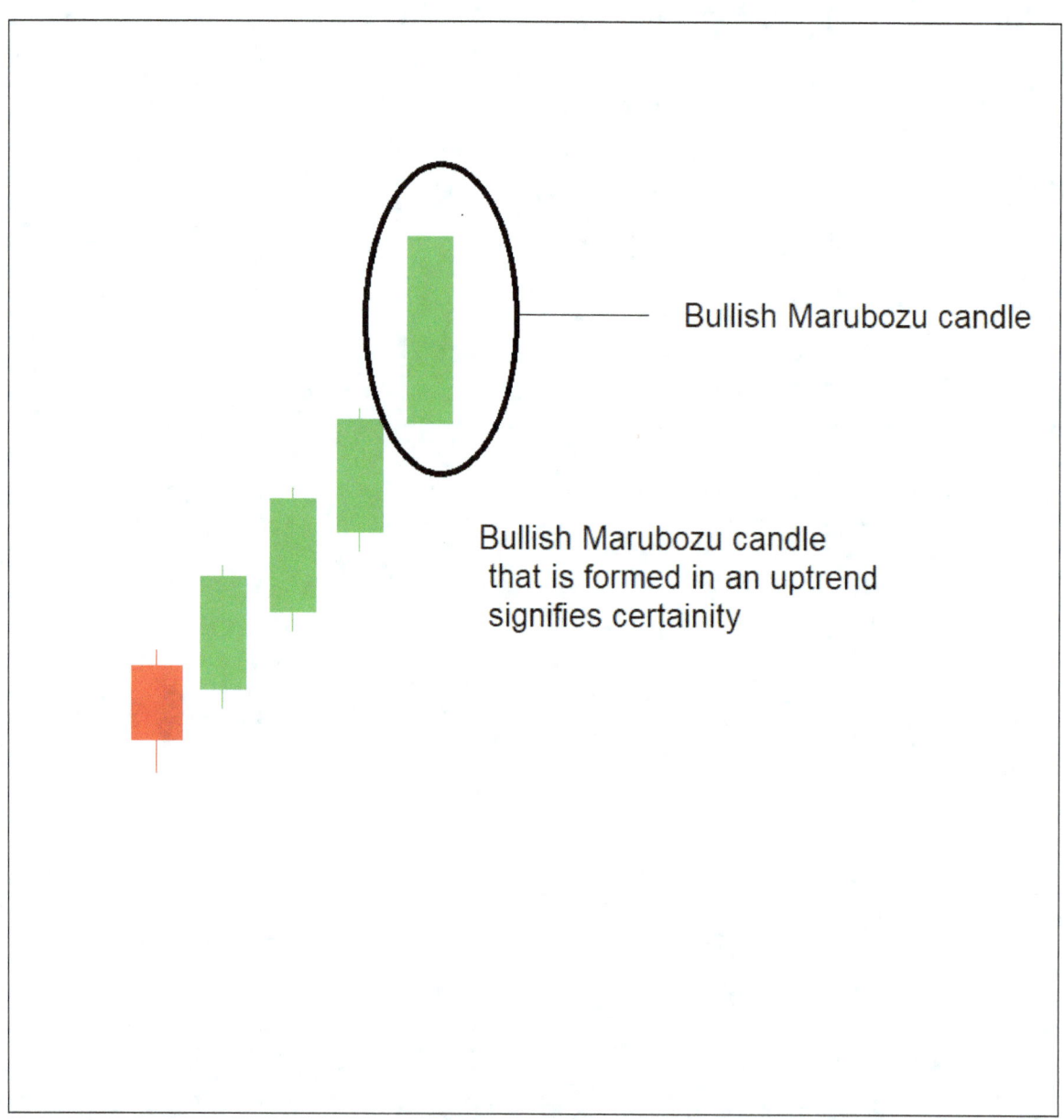

Bullish Marubozu candle

Bullish Marubozu candle
that is formed in an uptrend
signifies certainity

What is a Bullish Marubozu Pattern?

A Bullish Marubozu Pattern is a significant candlestick pattern in technical analysis that signals a strong buying momentum.

It is characterized by a long body with little or no wicks at both the upper and lower ends of the candle.

This pattern indicates that the bulls are in control, driving prices higher throughout the entire trading period.

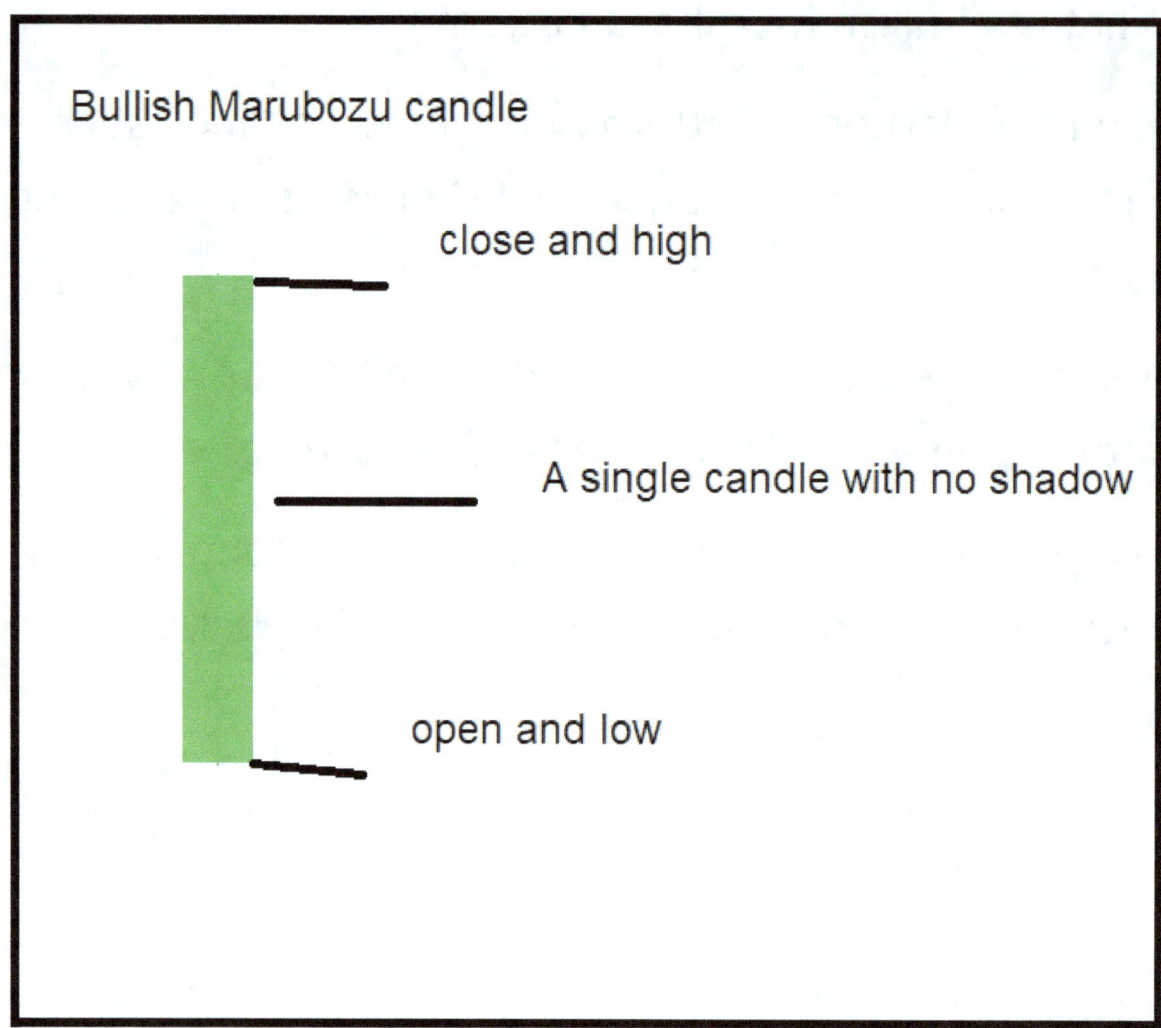

Bullish Marubozu candle

close and high

A single candle with no shadow

open and low

How does the Bullish Marubozu Pattern form?

The market opens- the trading session begins, and the opening price is relatively low, with the bears losing control of the market.

Buying momentum- the bulls take over and drive the price up, creating a strong upward trend throughout the trading session.

No significant pullbacks- during the formation of a Bullish Marubozu pattern, there are little to no significant pullbacks, as the bulls maintain their control.

The market closes- the trading session ends, and the closing point is very close to the highest point of the session. This demonstrates the strength of the bulls and their ability to maintain control.

Important points

Confirmation- A Bullish Marubozu on its own is not a guarantee of a continued upward trend. It is crucial to wait for additional confirmation, such as another bullish candlestick pattern or an upward breakout on high volume.

Context- Bullish Marubozu is more significant when it appears after a down- trend or a support level, as it suggests a potential trend reversal or bounce off the support level.

Volume- higher trading volume during the formation of a Bullish Marubozu Pattern indicates strong buying pressure adds credibility to the pattern.

Risk management – As with any trading strategy, it is crucial to use proper risk management techniques, such as stop-loss orders, to protect your investment in case the market moves against your position.

4. Bearish Marubozu Pattern:-

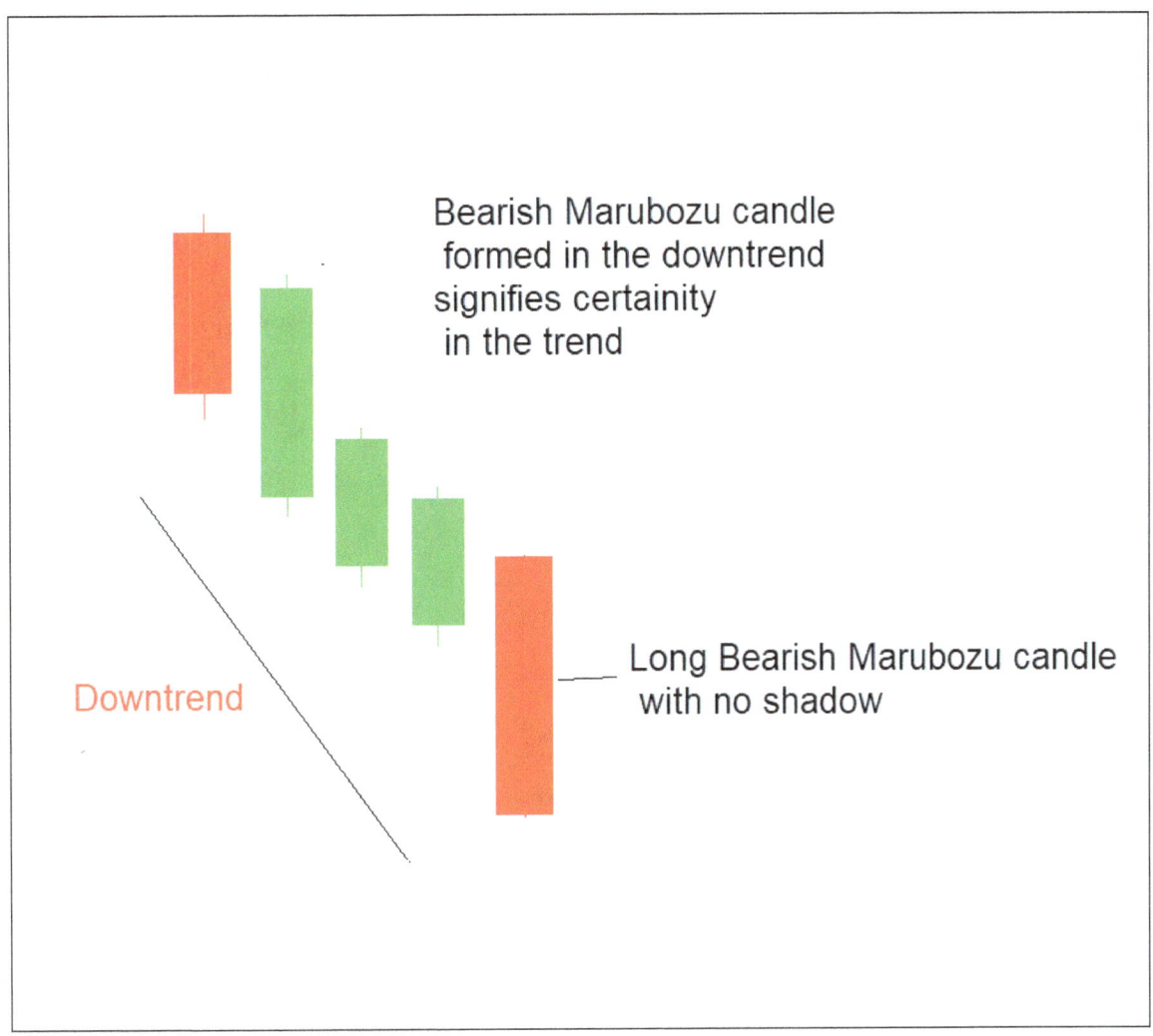

Bearish Marubozu candle
formed in the downtrend
signifies certainity
in the trend

Downtrend

Long Bearish Marubozu candle
with no shadow

What is a Bearish Marubozu Pattern?

A Bearish Marubozu Pattern is a single candlestick pattern that occurs in financial markets analysis to identify potential trend reversals or the continuation of a downtrend.

The pattern signifies strong selling pressure and a potential bearish outlook for the security in question.

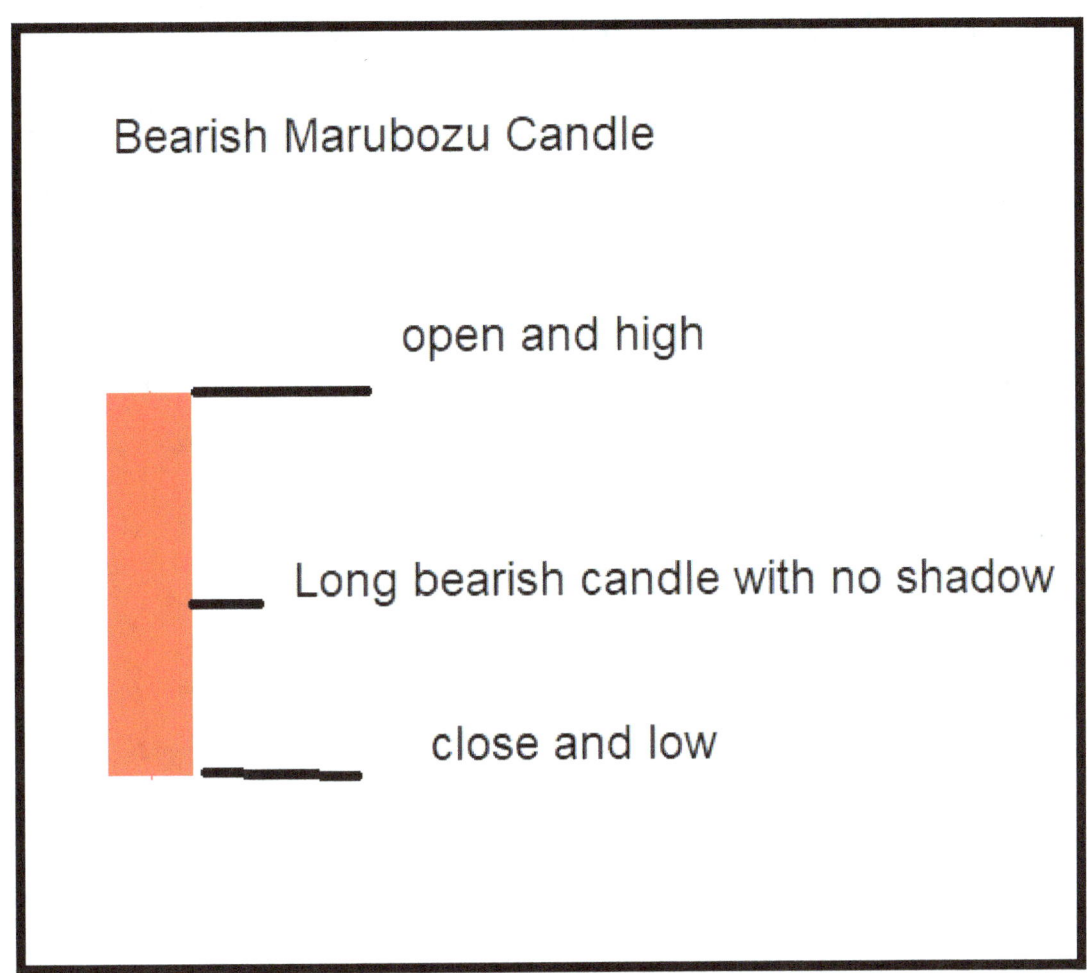

Bearish Marubozu Candle

open and high

Long bearish candle with no shadow

close and low

How the Bearish Marubozu Pattern forms-

The candlestick has a long body without upper and lower shadows. This means that open price was the high of the day, and close price was the low of the day.

The pattern usually appears after an uptrend or during a consolidation phase, suggestion a potential trend reversal or continuation of the downtrend.

Important points-

Confirmation- it is essential to wait for additional confirmation, such as a lower close on the next trading day or another bearish pattern, before making trading decisions based on the Bearish Marubozu Pattern.

Volume – high trading volume during the formation of the Bearish Marubozu Pattern indicates a stronger bearish sentiment and can add credibility to the pattern.

Context – the Bearish Marubozu Pattern should be analyzed within the context of the overall market trend, support and resistance levels, and other technical indicators to ensure a more accurate assessment of the market direction.

Risk management – as with any trading strategy, if is crucial to implement proper risk management techniques such as stop-loss orders and position sizing to minimum potential losses.

Remember, no single technical pattern guarantees success in trading, and the Bearish Marubozu Pattern should be used in conjunction with other tools and techniques for a comprehensive approach to market analysis.

5. Tweezer Top Pattern:-

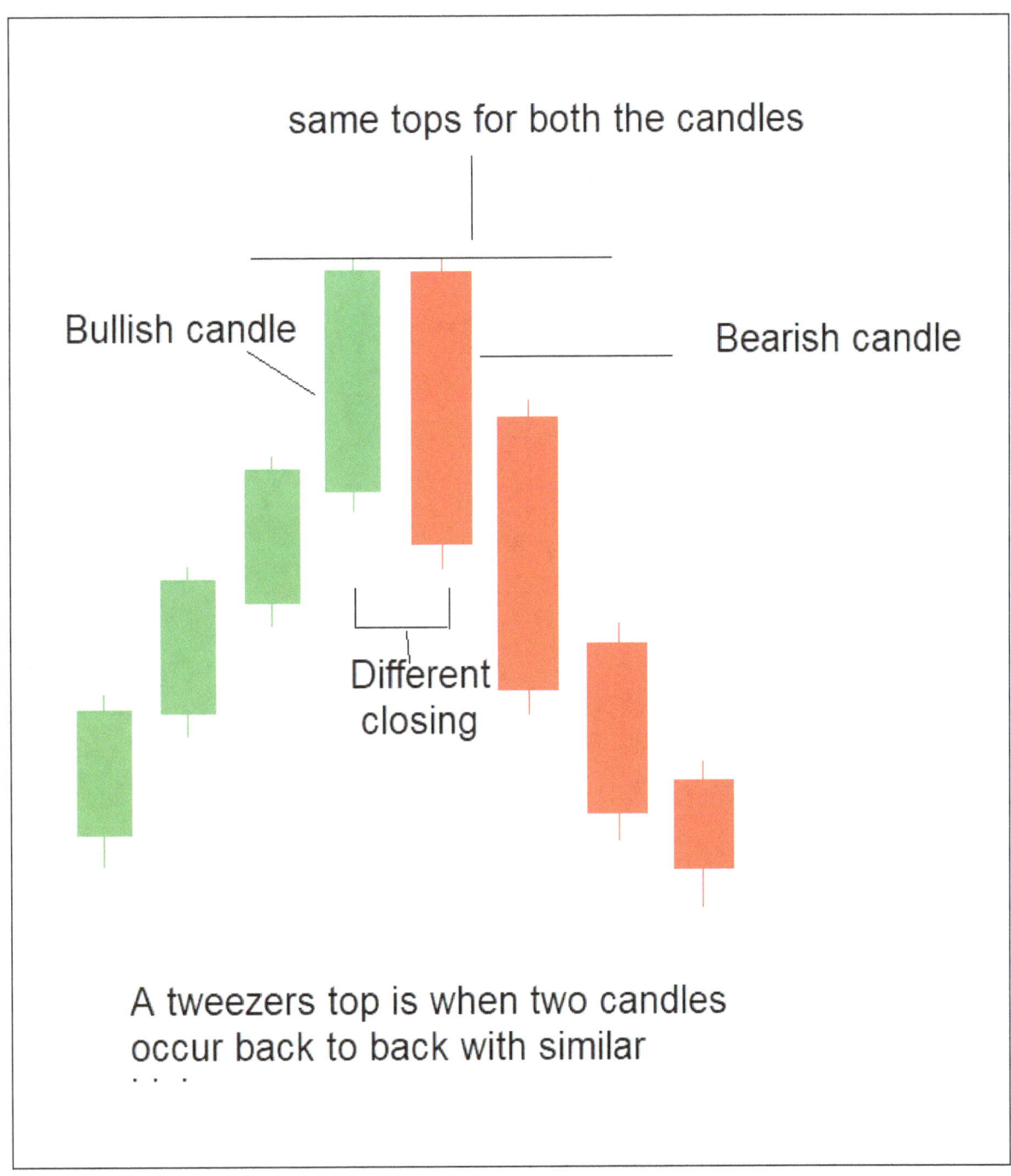

same tops for both the candles

Bullish candle

Bearish candle

Different closing

A tweezers top is when two candles occur back to back with similar

What is Tweezer Top Pattern?

A Tweezer Top Pattern is a bearish reversal pattern found in technical analysis of financial markets, typically observed in candlestick charts for stocks, commodities, or currencies.

It consists of two or more candlestick with matching highs, indicates a potential end to an uptrend and the start of a downtrend movement.

Tweezer Tops

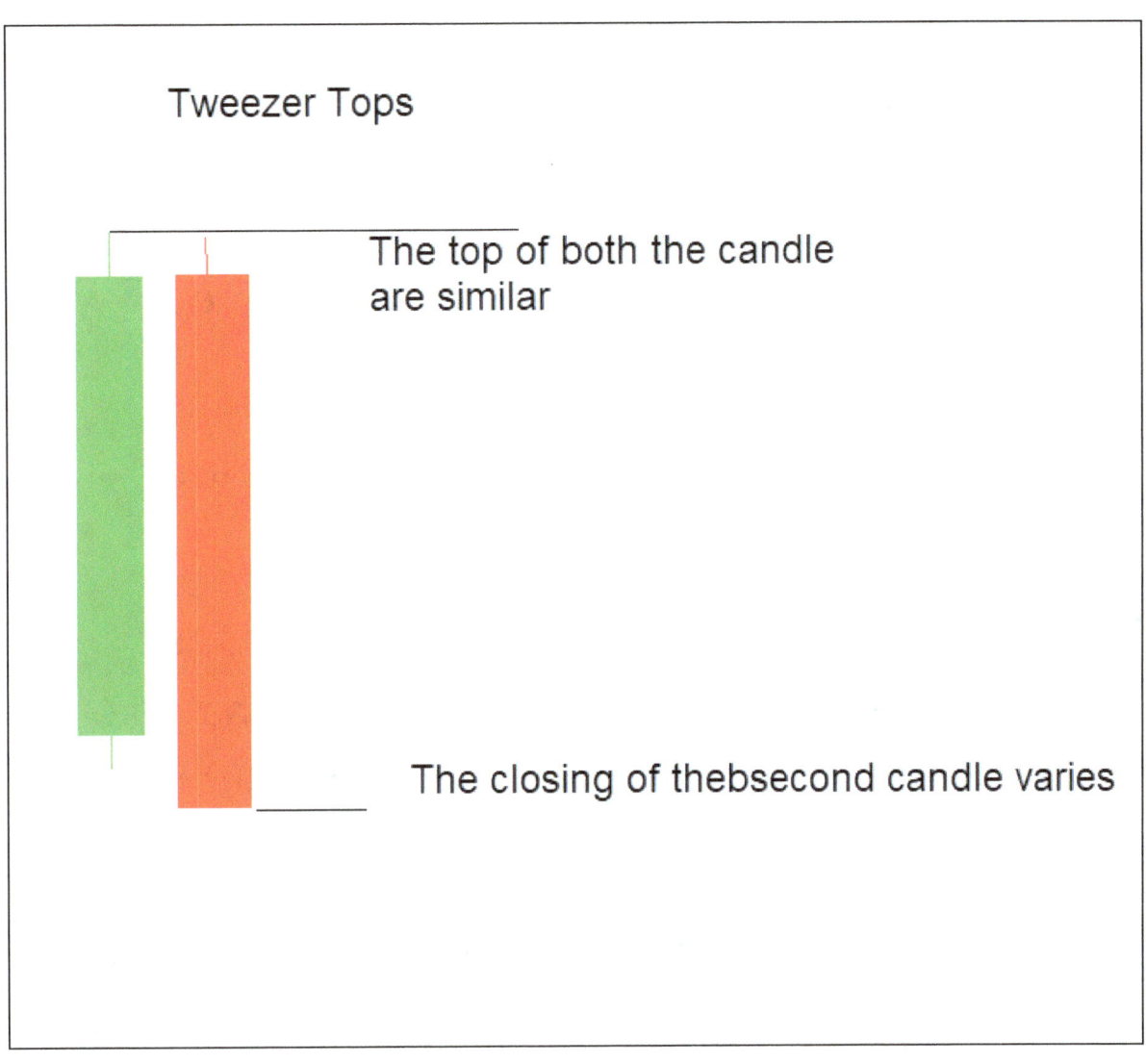

The top of both the candle are similar

The closing of thebsecond candle varies

The Tweezer Top Pattern forms in the following manners

An upward trend is in progress, with the market experiencing higher highs and higher lows.

A candlestick with a long upper shadow appears, suggesting strong selling pressure at the top.

The next candlestick has a similar high to the first candlestick, with upper shadows indicating that the market is struggling to break through a specific resistance level.

The inability to push past the resistance level signifies that buyers are losing control, and sellers are gaining momentum.

Important point-

Confirmation- the Tweezer Top Pattern is considered more reliable if it is followed by a bearish candlestick or another reversal pattern, confirming the shift in momentum.

Volume- a higher volume on the bearish candlestick following the Tweezer top can strengthen the pattern's credibility,

Support and resistance levels- the Tweezer Top Pattern should appear near a known resistance level, making it more significant as a potential reversal signal.

The preceding trend- the pattern should be preceded by a clear uptrend, as it is a bearish reversal pattern.

The number of matching highs- while the pattern can form with just two matching highs, it is considered more reliable if there are three or more candlestick with similar highs, as it shows a stronger resistance level.

Keep in mind that no pattern guarantees a market reversal, and traders should use additional technical analysis tools and risk management strategies to confirm signals and protect their positions.

6. Classic Doji Pattern:-

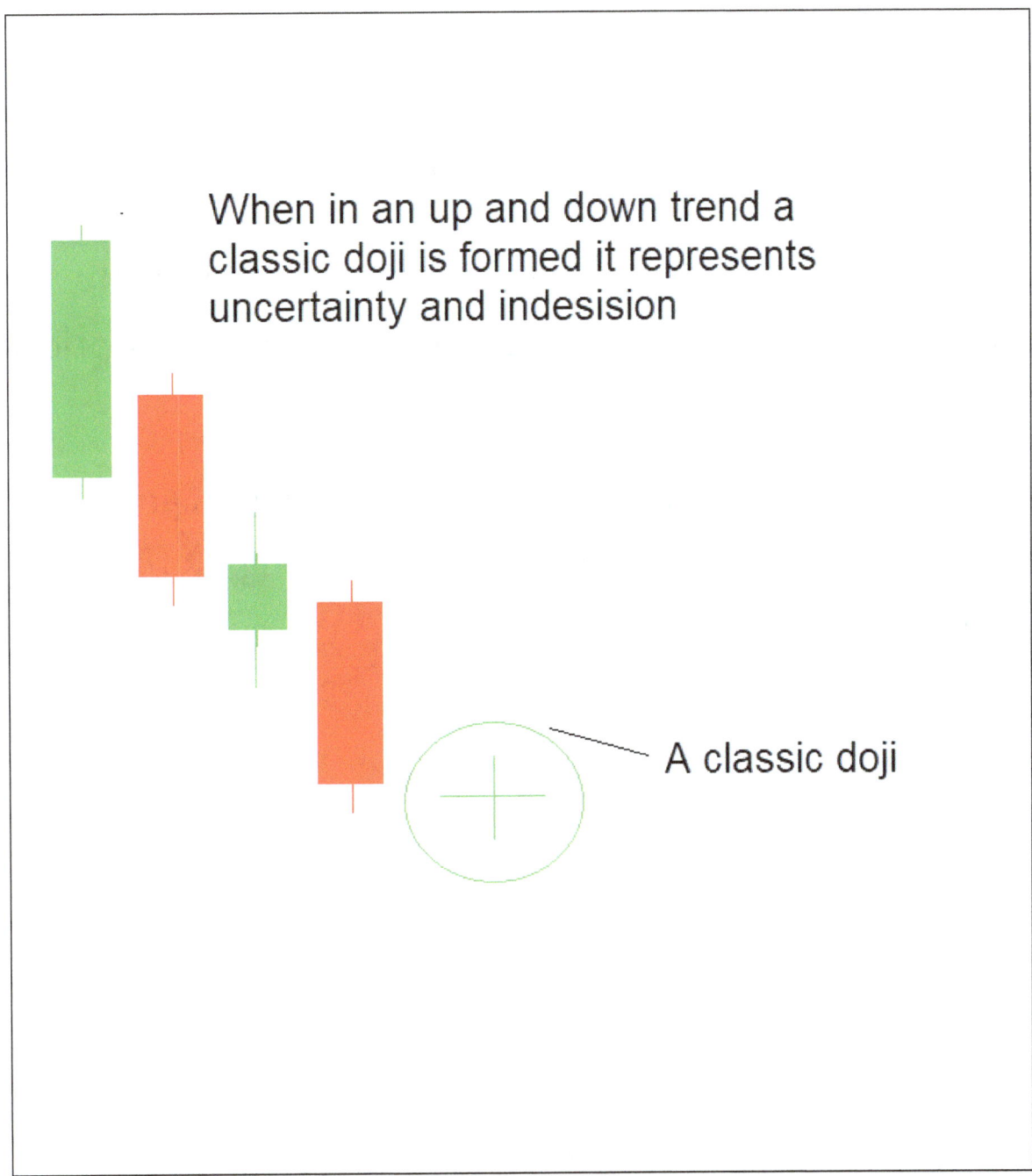

When in an up and down trend a classic doji is formed it represents uncertainty and indesision

A classic doji

What is a Classic Doji Pattern?

A Classic Doji Pattern is a candlestick pattern used in the technical analysis of financial markets, such as stocks, commodities and Forex.

It is characterized by a candlestick with a very small or nonexistent body and long upper and lower shadows.

The pattern signifies a period of indecision between buyers and sellers, where the opening and closing prices are almost equal.

It is considered a neutral pattern, potentially signaling a trend reversal or a continuation, depending on the context.

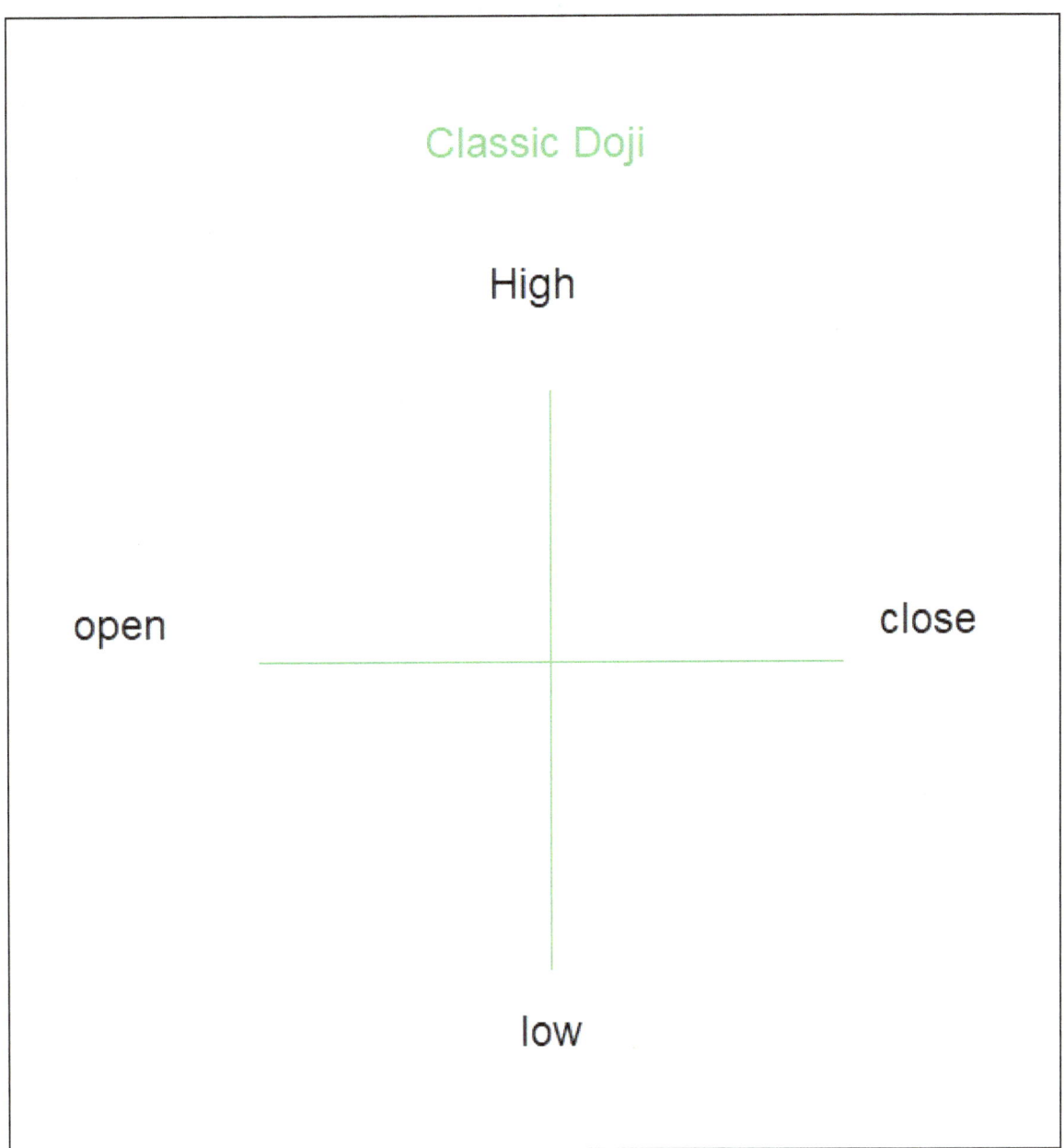

How does the Classic Doji Pattern form?

The Classic Doji Pattern forms when the markets opens, moves in a certain direction during the trading session, but then retraces back to close near the opening prices.

This indicates that neither buyers nor sellers could maintain control, resulting in a standoff.

Important points:-

Context-The Classic Doji Pattern is more significant when it appears a prolonged trend (either bullish or bearish) as it may indicate exhaustion and potential trend reversal. However, when it appears in a ranging market, it is less significant.

Confirmation- The Classic Doji Pattern should be used in conjunction with other technical analysis tools, such as support and resistance levels, trend-lines.

Volume- Analyzing trading volume during the formation of a Classic Doji Pattern can provide additional insight.

Keep in mind that no single technical analysis tool or pattern is foolproof. It is essential to use the Classic Doji Pattern in conjunction with other technical analysis tools and methods to improve your overall trading strategy.

7. Tweezer Bottom Pattern:-

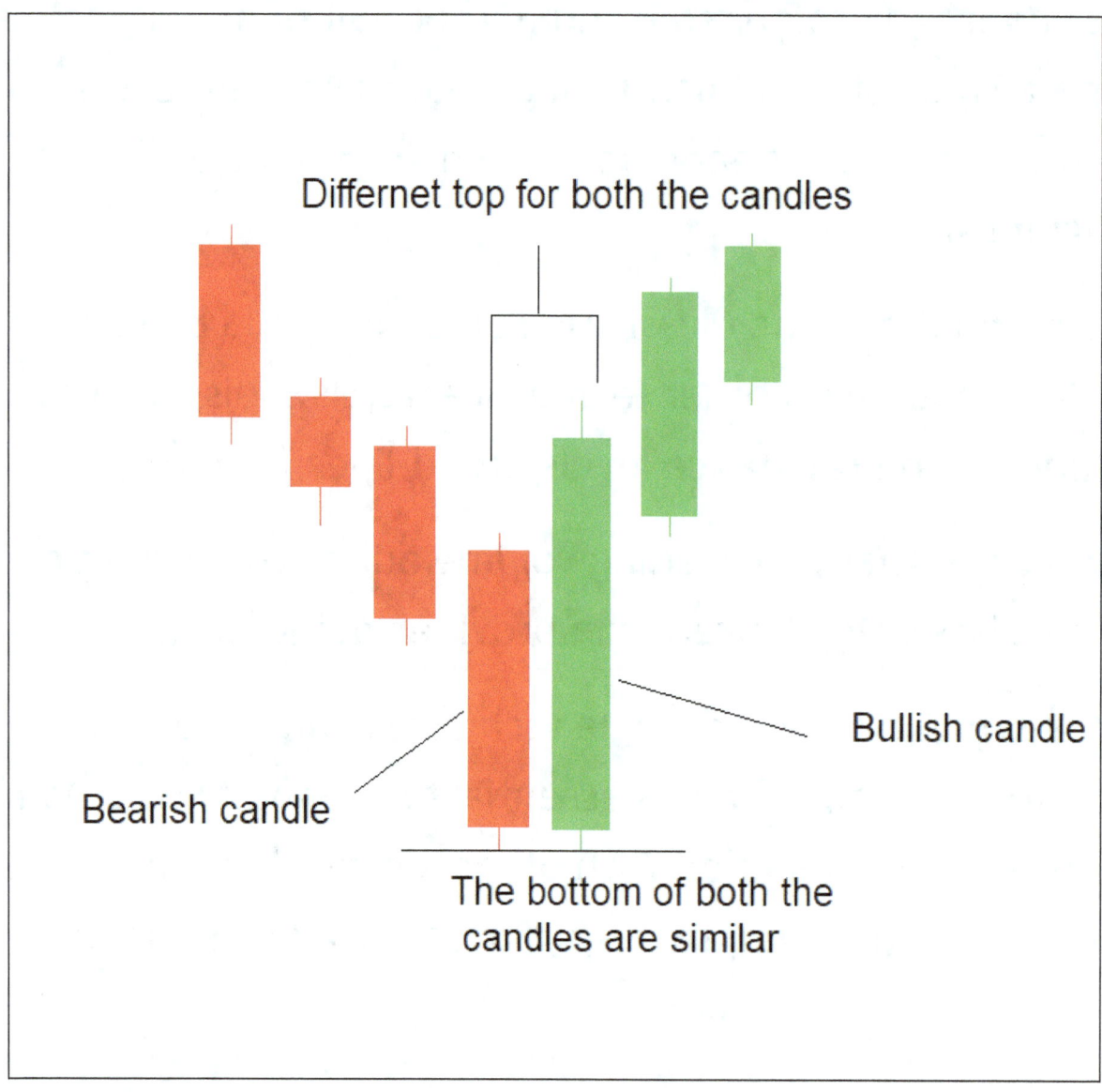

What is Tweezer Bottom Pattern?

A Tweezer Bottom Pattern is a bullish reversal candlestick pattern that occurs at the end of a downtrend or during a consolidation period.

It signals that the bears are losing control, and the bulls are gaining strength, which could result in a potential upward price movement.

The pattern consists of two or more candles, with the lows or these candles being equal or very close to each other.

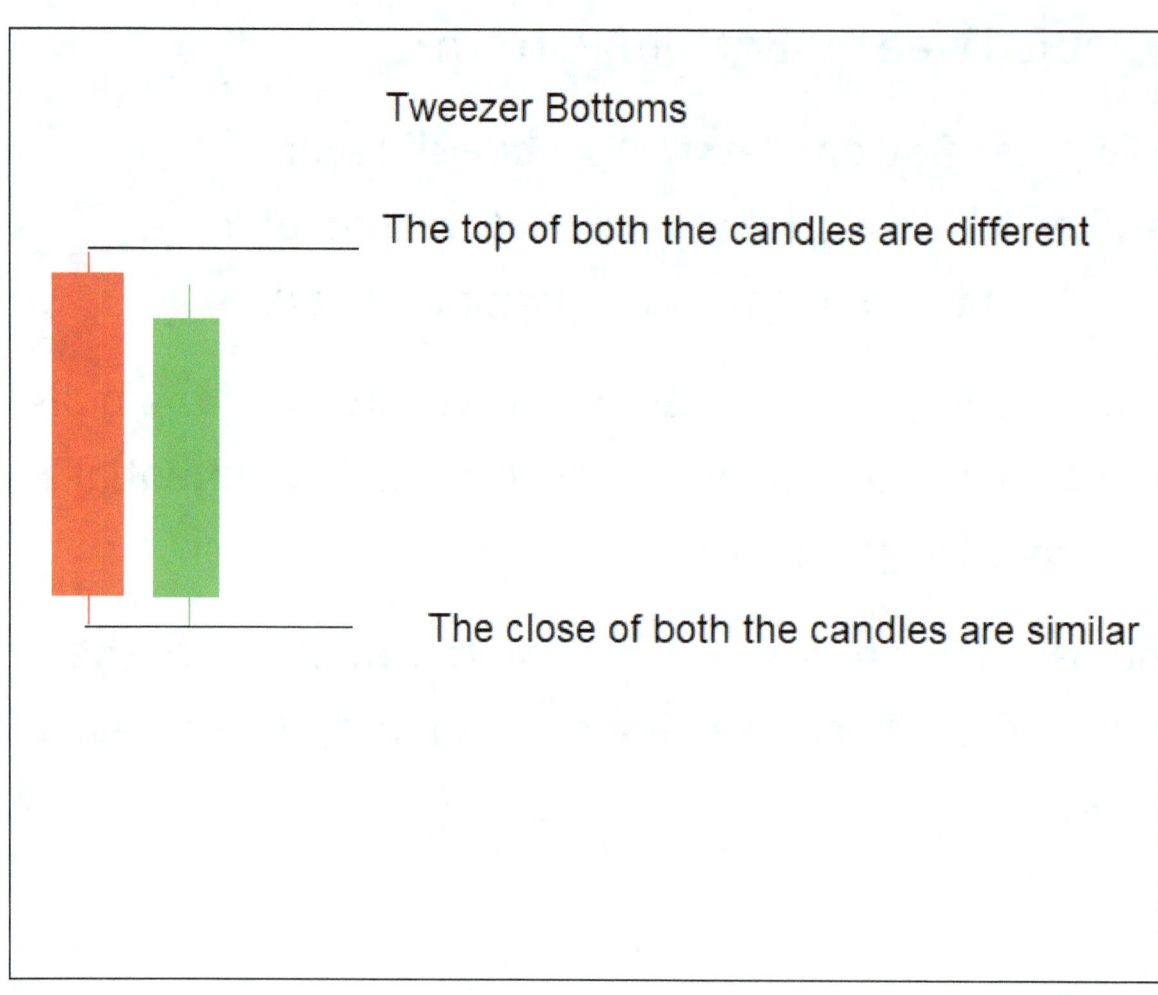

Tweezer Bottoms

The top of both the candles are different

The close of both the candles are similar

Formation of the Tweezer Bottom Pattern-

Downtrend or consolidation – the pattern appears after a downtrend or a period of consolidation, showing that the selling pressure is weakening.

First candle- the first candle in the pattern is a bearish candle with a relatively long body, indicating that the bears are still in control.

Second candle- the second candle is a bullish candle with a body equal of long to the previous candle, lows of both the candle are equal but high of second candle is more than first candle, indicates that the bears are unable to push the price lower.

Reversal - Tweezer Bottom Pattern is confirmed when the price moves higher after the Tweezer Bottom Pattern is formed, suggesting a reversal in the market sentiment.

Important Points-

The Tweezer Bottom Pattern is more reliable when it appears near support levels, such as trend-lines or moving averages, as these areas tend to act as a natural barrier for further downtrend movement.

The pattern gains strength if it is accompanied by high trading volume on the second bullish candle or if other technical indicators support the bullish reversal.

Remember that no pattern guarantees a 100% success rate, so always use the Tweezer Bottom Pattern in conjunction with other technical analysis tools to increase the probability of successful trades.

8. Long Legged Doji Pattern:-

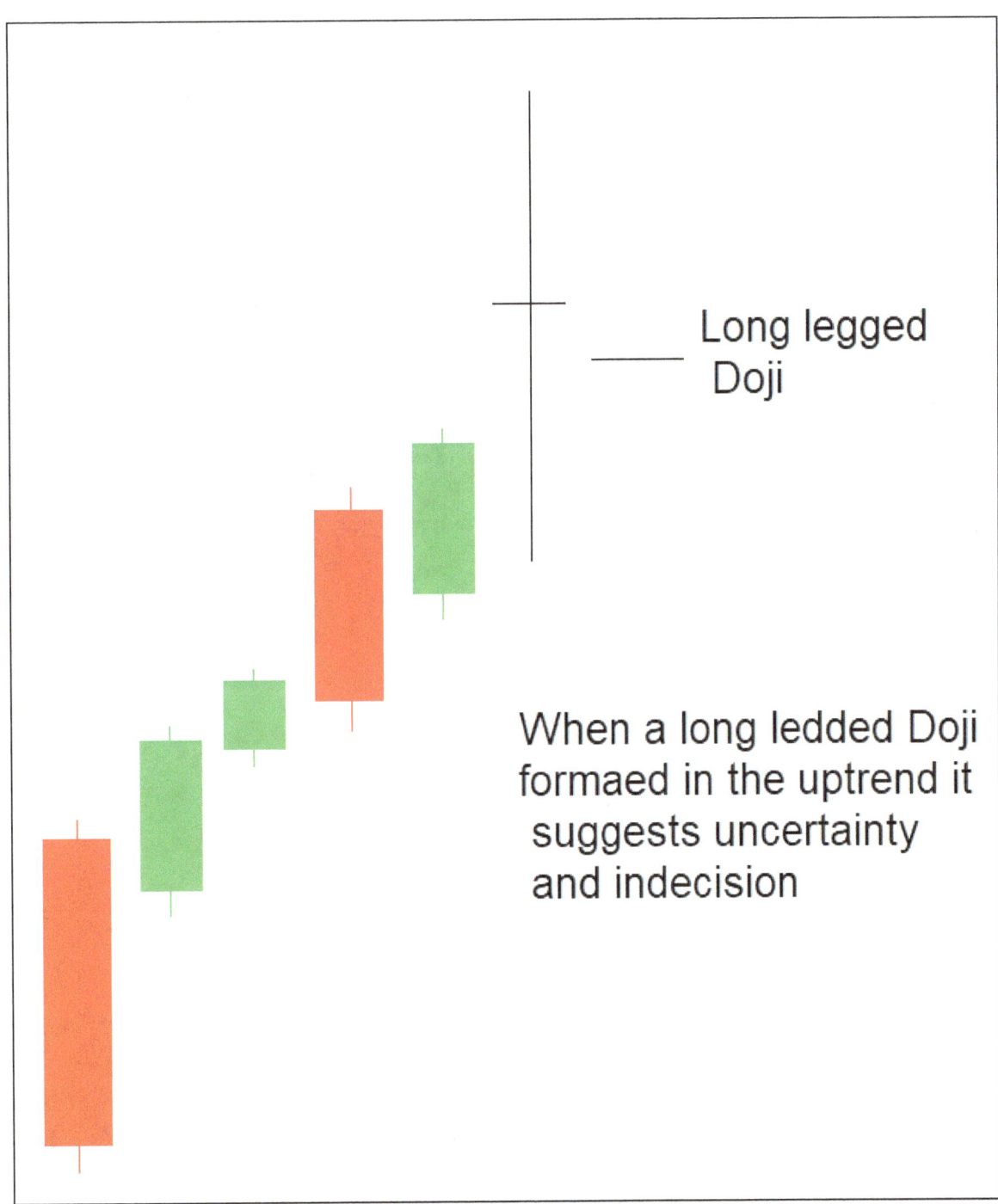

Long legged Doji

When a long ledded Doji formaed in the uptrend it suggests uncertainty and indecision

What is long legged Doji Pattern?

A long legged Doji Pattern is a candlestick pattern used in technical analysis to identify potential trend reversals or market indecision.

The pattern consists of a single candlestick with long upper and lower shadows and a very small body.

The opening and closing price of the candlestick are almost equal, which is why the body is small, and it represents the indecision in the market.

Long legged Doji

High

open and close are similar

Low

Formation of the long legged Doji Pattern-

The long legged Doji Pattern forms when there is significant price movement during a trading period, but the market ultimately closes near the opening price.

This can be interpreted as both the bulls and bears fighting for control, but neither gaining a clear advantage.

The long upper and lower shadows indicate that there was a wide trading range during the period, with prices moving significantly higher and lower before returning to a level close to the opening price.

Important points:

A long legged Doji Pattern can signal potential trend reversals or market indecision, but it is not a confirmation of a trend change. It is important to look for additional confirmation signals, such as other candlestick patterns, technical indicators, or price action analysis, to validate the potential reversal.

The pattern is more significant when it appears after a strong uptrend or downtrend, as it suggests that the momentum might be shifting or stalling.

The longer the shadows, the more indecision is present in the market, and the more significant the pattern may be. However, the length of the shadows should be compared to the shadows of the surrounding candlesticks to determine if the pattern is truly notable.

Always use the long legged Doji Pattern in conjunction with other technical analysis tools and within the context of the overall market trend to make informed trading decisions.

9. Hanging Man Pattern:-

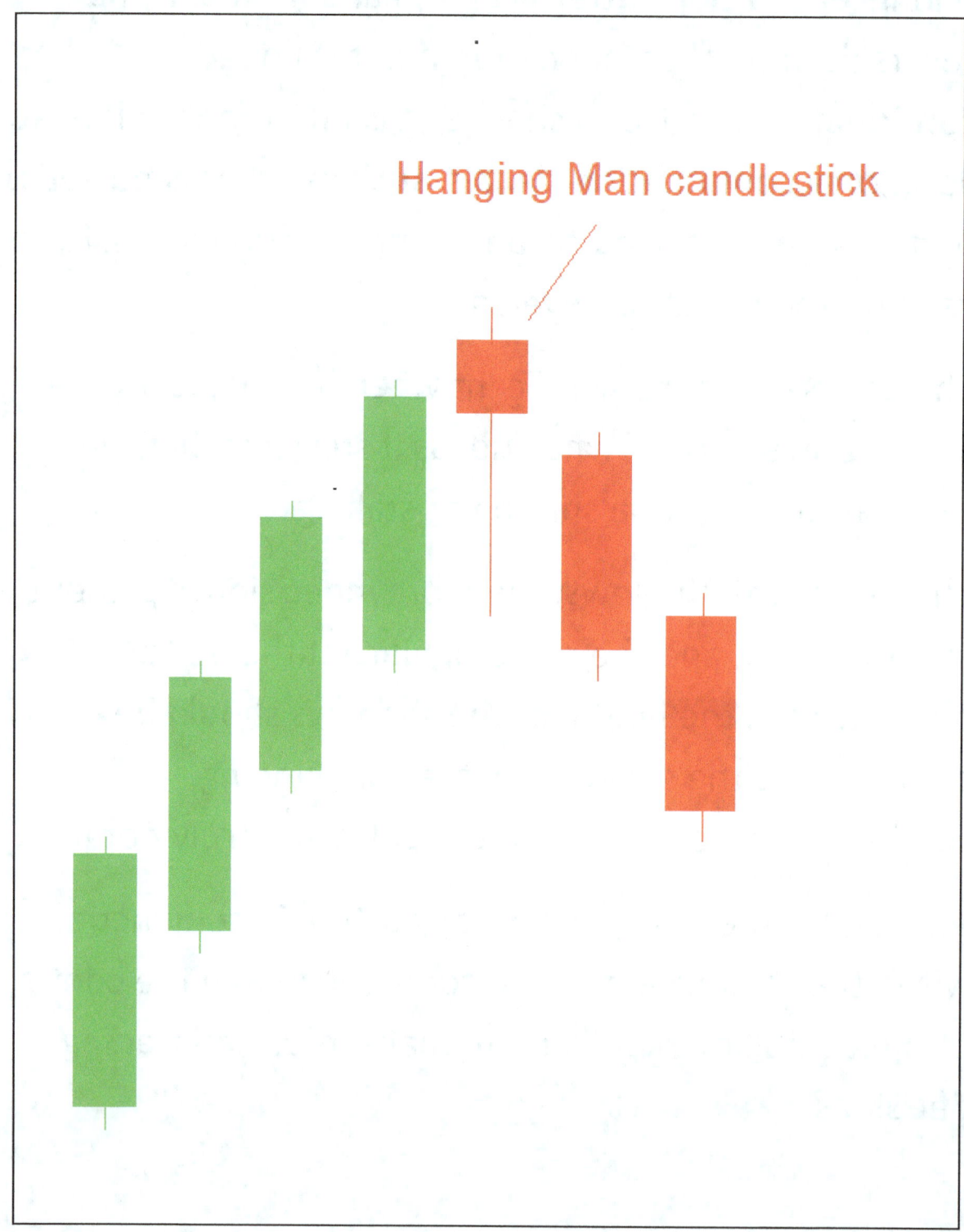

Hanging Man candlestick

What is Hanging Man Pattern?

The Hanging Man Pattern is a bearish reversal pattern in the field of technical analysis of price patterns in securities, most notably in stocks and forex.

It appears at the end of an uptrend and warns of a potential downtrend in prices. Here's description of how it forms and some of its key features.

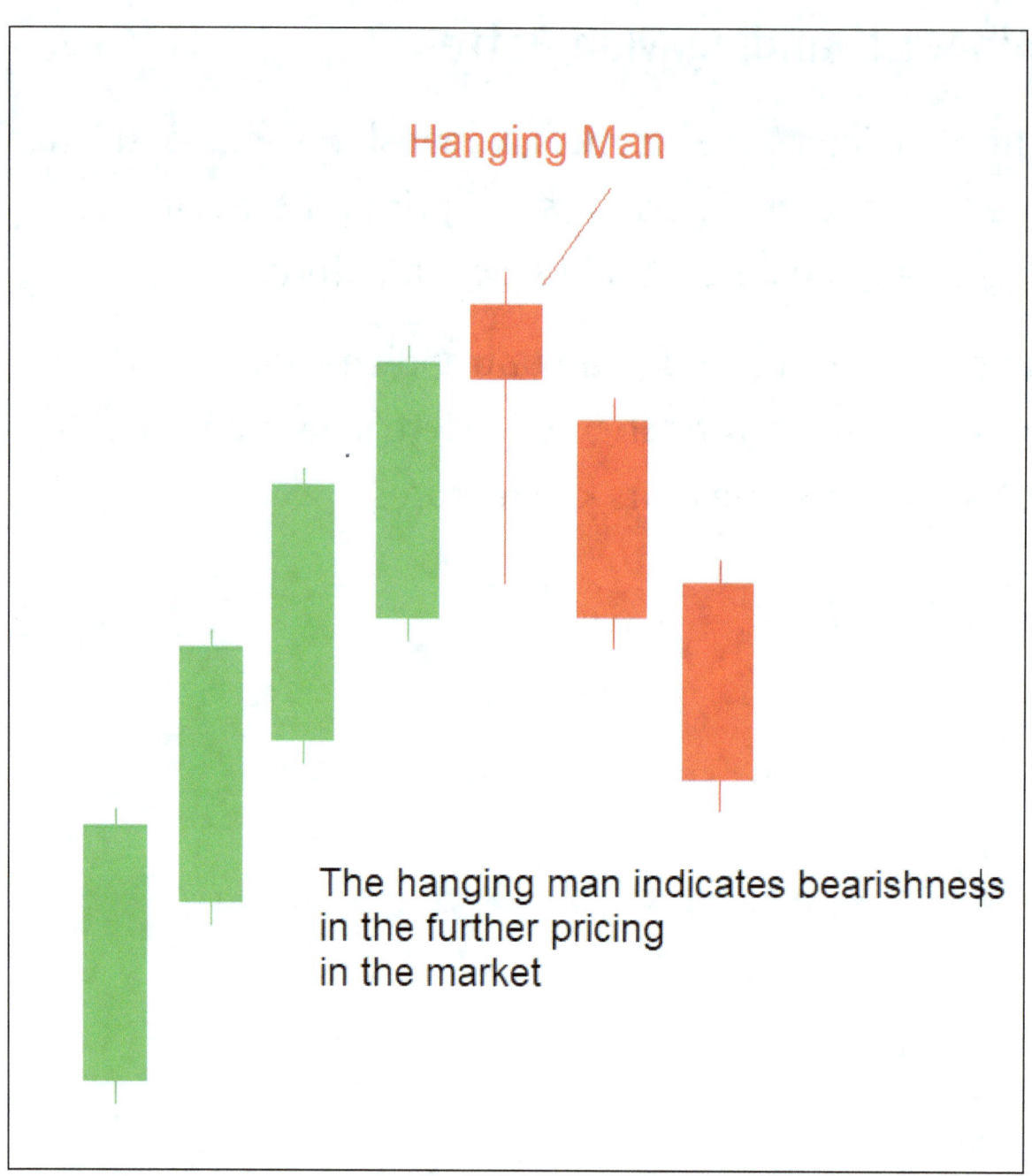

Hanging Man

The hanging man indicates bearishness
in the further pricing
in the market

How Hanging Man Pattern forms:

Uptrend – the Hanging Man Pattern appears during an uptrend, when prices have been increased.

Long lower shadow- The pattern itself forms on a day when the security opens, than trades significantly lower during the day, but then rallies to close near the opening price. This forms a 'candlestick' with a small body at the top and a long lower shadow, which looks a little like a hanging man.

Important points-

Confirmation is required- The Hanging Man Pattern indicates the potential for a reversal, but it should be used in conjunction with other indicators to confirm the reversal. A common practice is to wait for a bearish candlestick on the following day to confirm the reversal.

The length of the lower shadow- The lower shadow should be at least twice the length of the real body of the candlestick. The longer the lower shadow, the more significant the pattern is considered to be.

Upper shadow- The Hanging Man Pattern typically has little or no upper shadow.

The preceding uptrend- The more pronounced the preceding uptrend, the more bearish the Hanging Man Pattern is considered to be.

The Hanging Man Pattern is just one of many different candlestick patterns that traders use to guide their decisions. It is essential to use it as part of a broader analytical framework rather than in isolation, because, like all technical indicators, it is not 100% reliable.

10. Inverted Hammer:-

Inverted Hammer

What is Inverted Hammer Pattern?

The Inverted Hammer Pattern is a type of candlestick pattern found in technical analysis of financial markets, which can potentially signal a bullish reversal in price trend.

This pattern is usually observed at the bottom of a downtrend and might indicate an upcoming bullish move.

The inverted hammer looks like a single candlestick with a long upper shadow, small real body located at the lower end, and a short or no lower shadow.

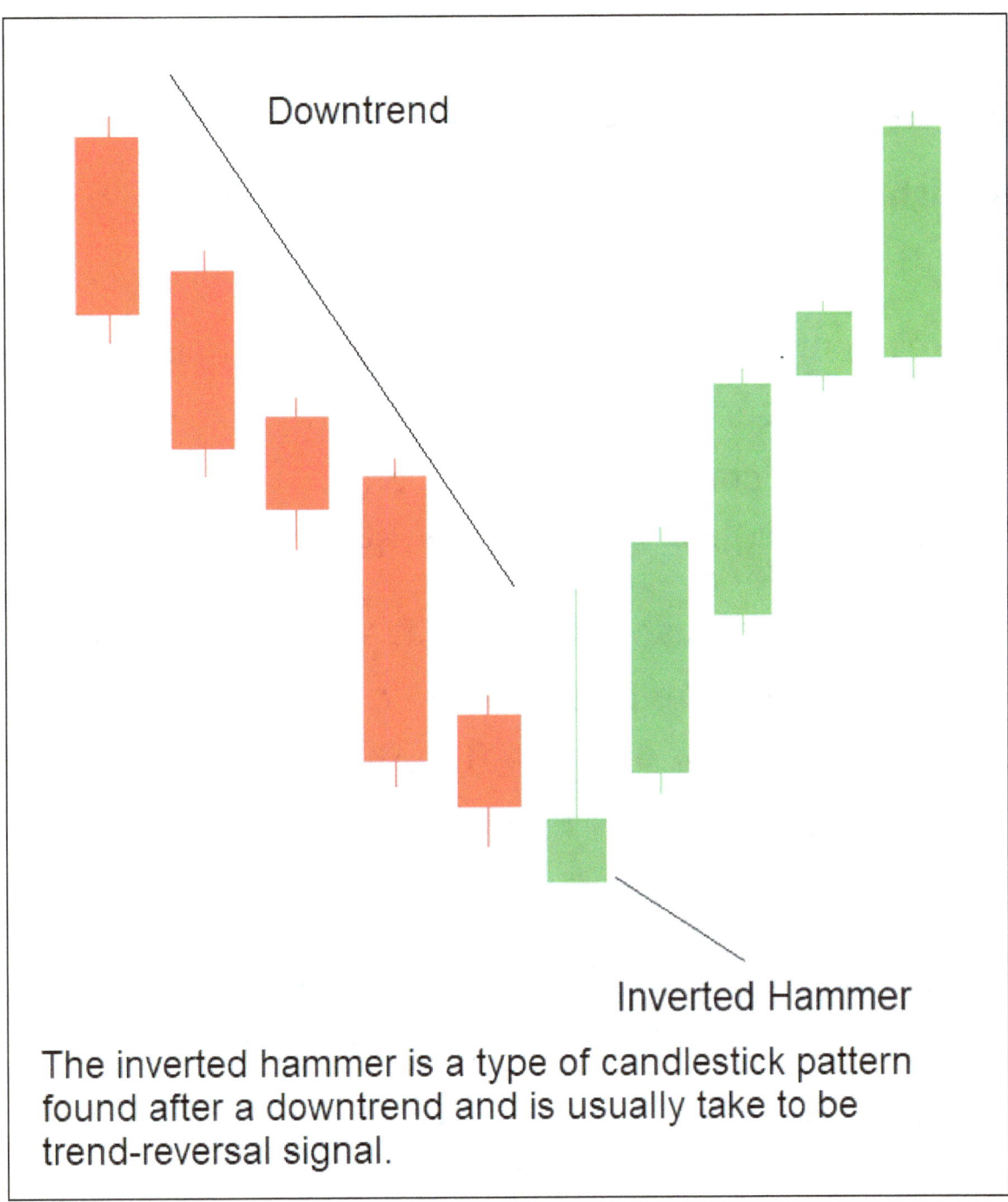

Downtrend

Inverted Hammer

The inverted hammer is a type of candlestick pattern found after a downtrend and is usually take to be trend-reversal signal.

How does the Inverted Hammer Pattern form?

Bearish Market- This pattern is first characterized by a downtrend or bearish market.

Market opening and initial downtrend movement- On the day the inverted hammer occurs, the market opens and price may continue to drop slightly, which indicates that sellers still have control over the market.

Buyer entry and push- however, at some point, buyers enter the market and push the price up. The rise, however, should be significantly larger than the initial downtrend movement. This results in a long upper shadow.

Resistance and close- the price rise in met resistance causing the price to fall again and close near to where it opened. This forms the small body of the candle at the bottom and a long upper shadow.

Short or no lower shadow- In most cases, the price does not go lower than the open, hence the short or no lower shadow.

Important point-

Confirmation – This pattern requires a confirmation to validate it as a bullish signal. The confirmation could be a gap up or long bullish candle, typically on the following day.

Long upper shadow- the upper shadow should be at least twice the height of the real body. This signifies that the buyers pushed the prices up significantly but could not sustain the upward momentum for the period.

Stop loss- In trading, it is important to have a stop-loss, a point where you accept your loss and exit the trade to prevent further loss. For the inverted hammer, it is usually placed a little below the low of the pattern.

Do not rely solely on this pattern- While the inverted hammer can be a powerful tool in technical analysis, it should not be used in isolation. Other technical indicators and the overall market context should also be considered to make the most accurate trading decisions.

11. Dragonfly Doji Pattern:-

Dragon fly Doji

What is Dragonfly Doji Pattern?

The Dragonfly Doji Pattern is a type of candlestick pattern that signals indecision and potential reversal in the current price trend.

It is particularly used in technical analysis of financial markets like stocks, forex, commodities.

Dragon Fly Doji

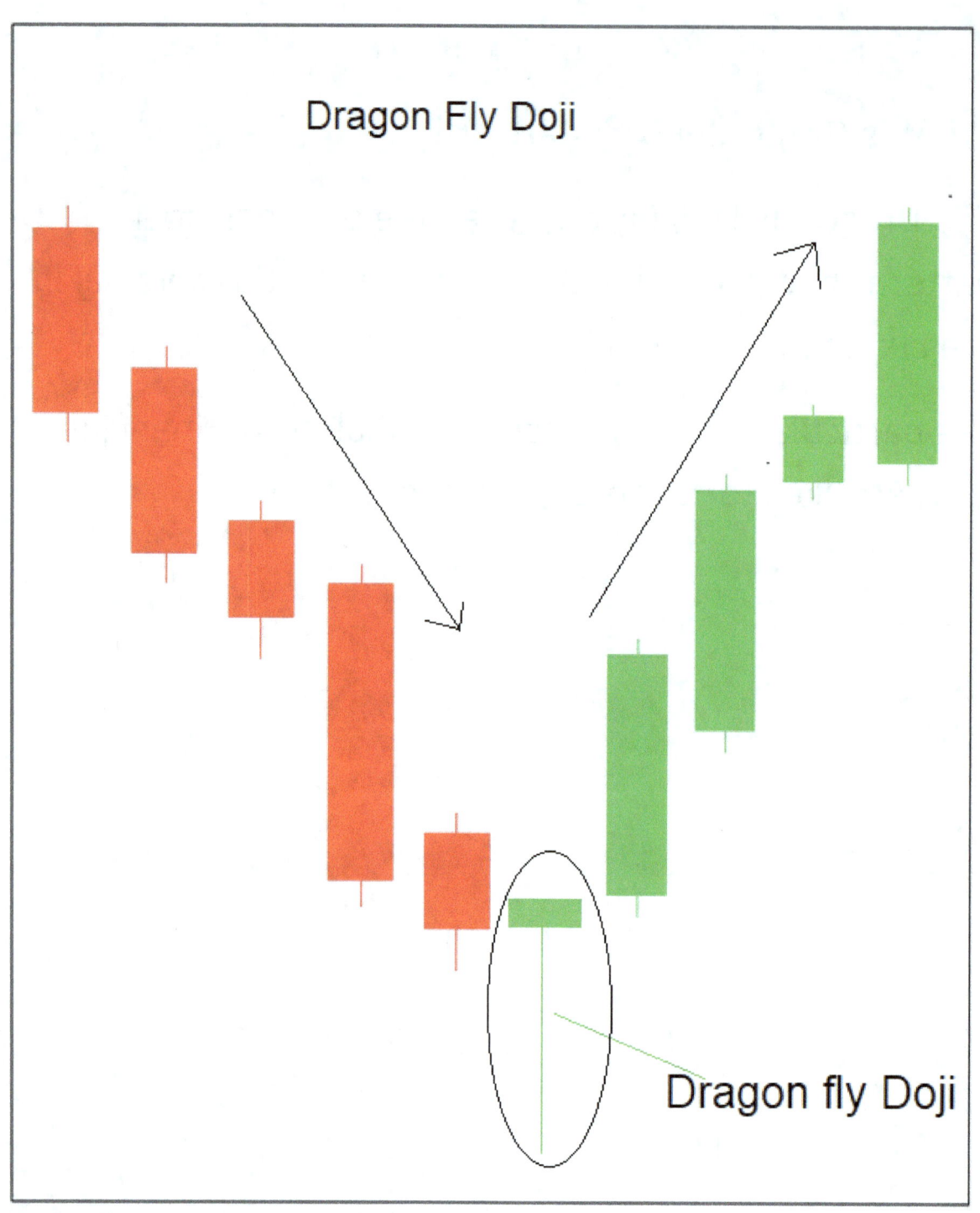

Dragon fly Doji

Formation of a Dragonfly Doji Pattern-

The Dragonfly Doji Pattern forms when the opening, closing and high prices are the same or about the same and the low price create a long lower shadow. It resembles the shape of a T.

It shows that sellers controlled the price action at the session, driving prices at the start of the session, driving prices lower, but by the end of the session, buyers were able to push the price back up to the opening price, indicating the potential for a bullish reversal.

How Dragonfly Doji Pattern forms in simple –

The market opens, and prices fall sharply during the session, which indicates strong selling pressure.

However, by the end of the session, the buyers step in and push the prices back up to where the market opened.

The session closes at or near the opening price, creating a candlestick with a very small body and a long shadow lower.

Important point about Dragonfly Doji Pattern-

Context- The Dragonfly Doji Pattern should be considered in conjunction with previous price action and future confirmation. Alone, it does not necessarily mean the trend will reverse, but in the context of a downtrend and followed by a bullish candle, it becomes a strong signal of potential bullish reversal.

Confirmation- Confirmation is usually required after a Dragonfly Doji Pattern to indicate a turn in the trend. This could be gap up or long bullish candlestick.

Shadow Length- The longer the lower shadow, the more significant the pattern can be as it indicates a bigger rejection of the lower prices.

Rare occurrence- the Dragonfly Doji Pattern is not a common pattern. Because it requires such specific conditions to form, it may not appear frequently. When it does, traders pay special attention to it.

Risk management- Like all trading signals, the Dragonfly Doji should be used in conjunction with other indicators and tools to manage risk and determine the best entry and exit points.

Remember that while the Dragonfly Doji and other candlestick patterns can provide insight into potential market reversals, they do not provide any guarantee. Always use sound risk management and trading discipline alongside technical analysis.

12. **Gravestone Doji Pattrn:-**

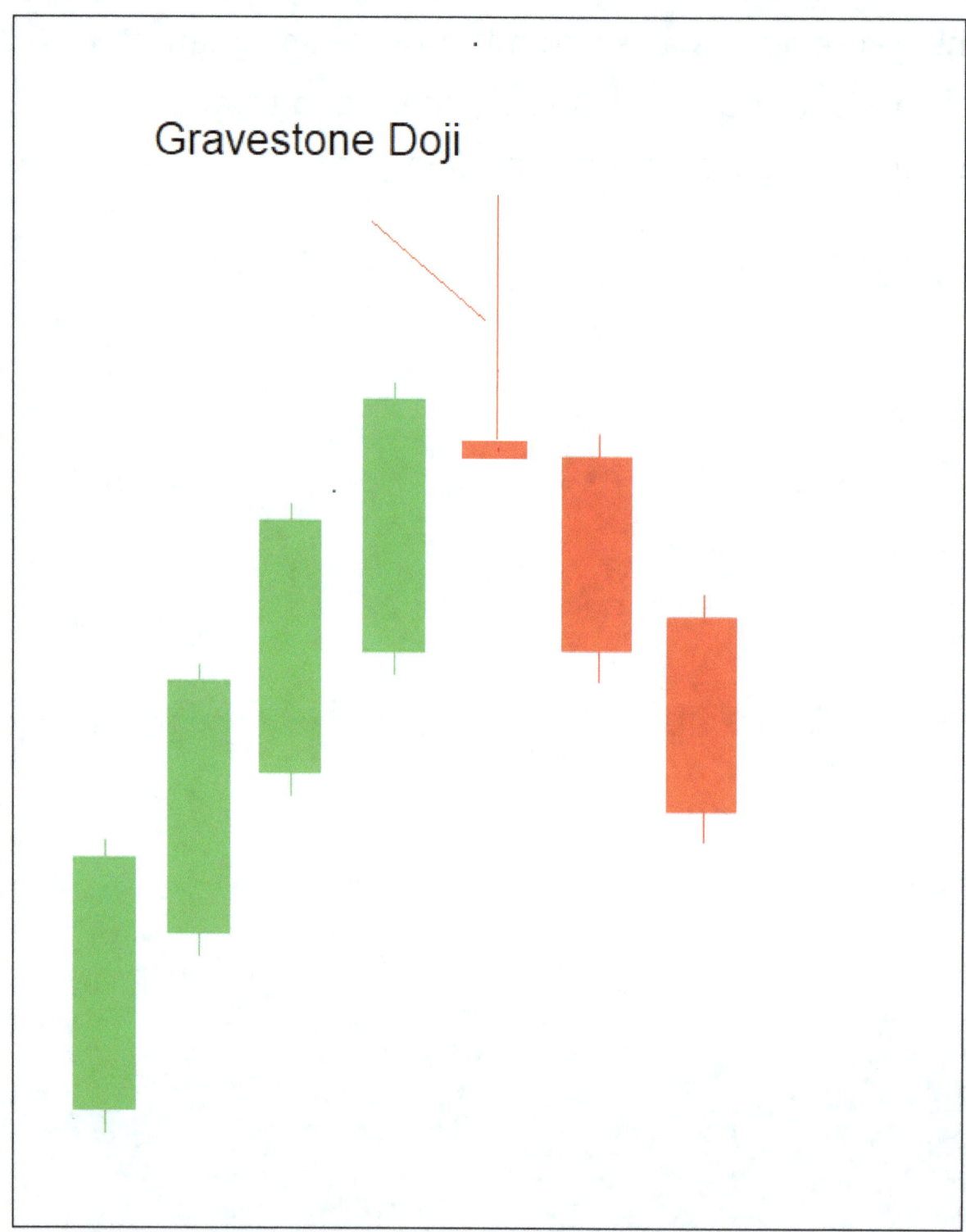

Gravestone Doji

What is Gravestone Doji Pattern?

A gravestone doji pattern is a type of candlestick pattern used in technical analysis to potentially predict a bearish reversal in the market.

It is a distinct pattern that signifies the failure of buyer to close the market at a higher level, thereby suggesting a change in the trend.

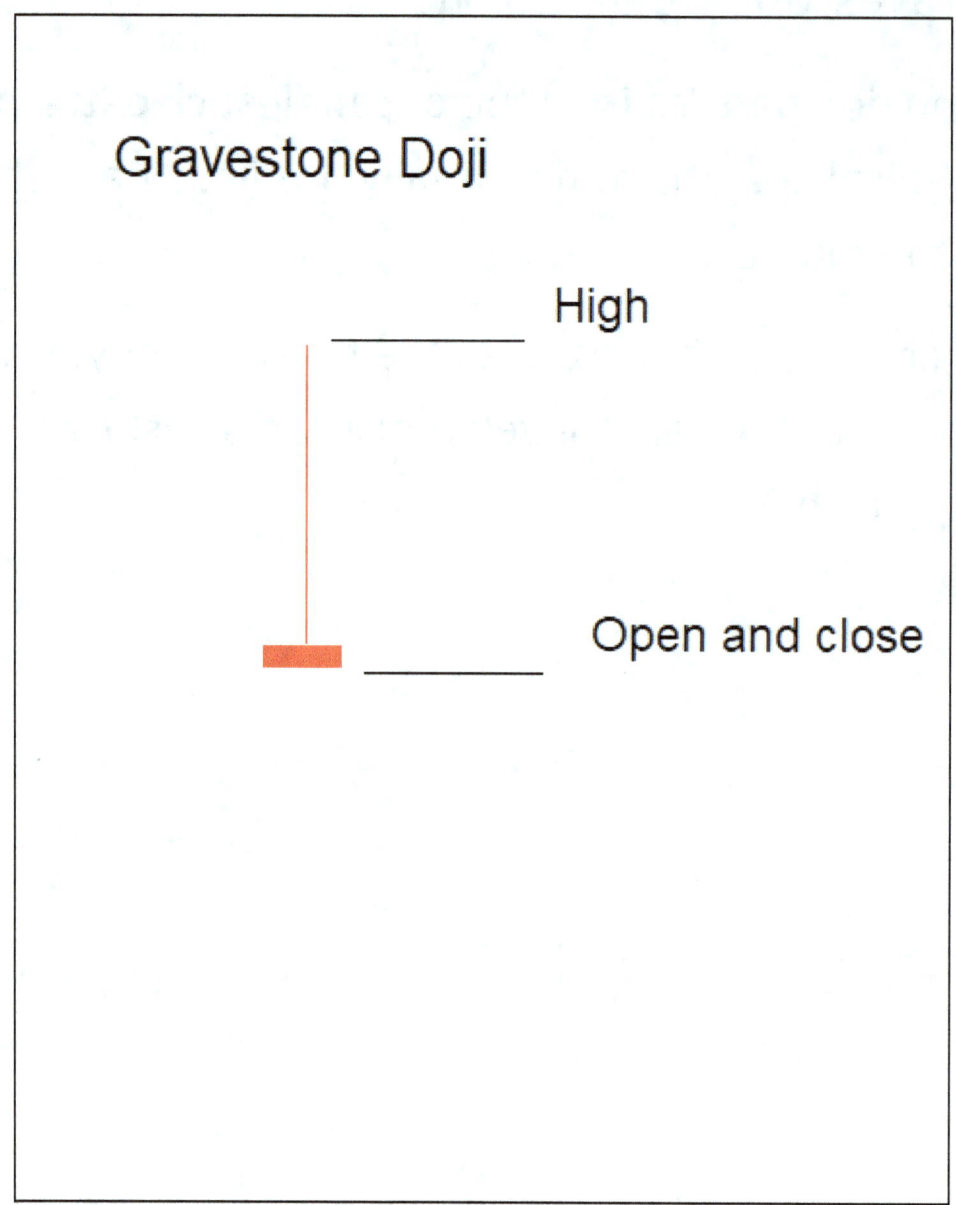

Gravestone Doji

High

Open and close

Formation of a Gravestone Doji Pattern-

A Gravestone Doji Pattern is formed when the open, close and low prices are the same, or about the same, with a long upper shadow and no, or very little, lower shadow. This results in a pattern that looks like a gravestone, hence the name. Here's more detailed step-by-step process:

The market opens and trade higher. The buyers push prices up, reflecting bullish sentiment.

However, by the end of the trading period, the market reverse and goes back to or near the opening price. This signals that the buyers couldn't maintain their position.

The result is a candlestick with a long upper shadow and little or no lower shadow, where the open, low and close prices are approximately the same.

Important points about Gravestone Doji Pattern-

Context- The pattern is significant when it appears after an uptrend or at a price resistance area. In isolation, it may not be a reliable indicator of future price movements.

Confirmation- while the Gravestone Doji can indicate a potential reversal. It's important to wait for confirmation in the form of a bearish candlestick in the following session or other confirming signals.

Volume- A higher volume on the day gravestone doji forms can provide further confirmation of a potential reversal. Increased volume shows more participation in the price move, making a reversal more likely.

Risk Management – Like all technical analysis tools, the gravestone doji is not foolproof and should be used in conjunction with other indicator and tools. Stop-loss orders and other risk management strategies should be used to protect against potential losses.

Pattern Variations- There can be minor variation in the gravestone doji pattern. For example, the open and close don't have to be exactly at the low of the day. As long as the open, low and close are near each other, and there is a long upper shadow, the pattern is generally considered a gravestone Doji.

Remember, it's important to use the gravestone doji pattern as part of a broader analysis of the market, rather than relying on it solely to make trading decisions.

Notes-

Notes-

Notes-